A Dictionary

of

ULSTER POSH SPEAK

compiled by

Billy Simpson

and

Doreen McBride

*A Phonetic Guide to Words and Phrases Thet Let
People Know You Hev a Bit of Kless*

Incorporating

The Cherryvelly Chronicles II

ADARE PRESS
White Gables
Ballymoney Hill
Banbridge
Telephone: (018206) 23782

ISBN 1 89946 04 1

A Catalogue record of this book is available from the British Library.

CONTENTS

ACKNOWLEDGEMENTS

We are indebted to a number of amateur social scientists, who share our delight in the poetry, rhythm and cadence of posh speak and who have, to the dismay of their friends and relatives, generously suggested words and phrases for inclusion in this dictionary. The words 'amateur' and 'generously' are not chosen randomly but for the purpose of conveying to our contributors that appreciation and gratitude is what you get instead of paid.

Some of those who have written to us have wisely chosen to remain anonymous while others have used names that might well be fictitious. In any event we would like to thank:

Carol Boyd

Tom Carson

Charlie McCormick

Sarah McBride

Roberta Hutchinson.

Trudy McClenaghan

'Hairy' from Donegall Pess

George McBride

Owen Kelly

And of course to Mrs. Egnes Johnston, her family and friends, without whom this book would not have been possible.

PREFACE

The success, last year, of our first book  *Talking Proper* (Adare Press, £3.99) has convinced us that, in a yobbish age, a great hunger exists for a touch of culture and good breeding — or at least the appearance of it.

We have had many letters from people who after reading *Talking Proper* are finding that they now cannot speak any other way, even after therapy.

It was encouragement like this which prompted us to produce this even fuller guide to talking proper, *The Dictionary of Ulster Posh Speak*. A study of these pages should help you acquire a manner of speech acceptable among the kind of people who attend the Grand Opera House even when there's an opera on.

You too can aspire to subsidised culture, a Volvo and a house with a name instead of a number and this book will help you sound as if you already have them.

The value of our work is perhaps best expressed by a lady who wrote to thank us for opening up a whole new world for her. She had 'Never seen a Belly before' and was inspired by our words to go to see 'Swan Lake' performed live. "Ay was epsolutely enreptured," writes E.K. of Belfast. "I cried may ays out. It was so sed when thet duck died thet ay couldn't look at orange sauce for a month efterwords."

No one could ask for a more touching testimonial.

POSH SPEAK – USEFUL WORDS

by Billy Simpson and Doreen McBride

Apart from Royalty, few English speakers today use 40's-speak but the tradition is still preserved in a few brave outposts of civilisation, including parts of this province and not just in such obvious places as the Malone Road, the Gold Coast of North Down, and of course Cherryvelly. The upholders of this cultural tradition are invariably women.

In speech with a touch of kless there are no 'common' words. Not if you say them right.

The main problem of compiling a posh speak dictionary is that the 'A' section would be non-existent. The 'Ah' sound is not acceptable and tends to be replaced by an 'E' or an 'O'.

For instance 'Abbey' is pronounced 'Ebbey' and 'Ardvark' is 'Ordvork'.

Even words that sound the same can have totally different meanings.

In speech with a touch of kless there are no 'common' words

For example – To most of us **toll** is what a bell does. But in posh speak it means over six foot.

Sten is not a gun but short for Stenley. As in, Sten Laurel end Oliver Hordy.

Flesh is not only the meaty part of people, it is an expression of great speed – as in it was all over in a flesh.

For instance, in few other places could **Hoard** be understood as the opposite of soft.

Or **Heff** regarded as fifty percent. Or 55 percent explained as Heff end a wee bit.

An **Ex** is, what lumberjecks cut down trees with.

Het is headwear.

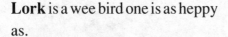

Het

A good ten

Lork is a wee bird one is as heppy as.

Ten is sunburn.

And **Tin** is a number between 9 and 11.

End means both also and finis. (What foreigners put at the end of their boring films).

Lork — little bird one is as heppy as

Beck is the opposite of front.

Bed has multiple definitions.
(1) The opposite of good.
(2) What one sleeps on et night.
(3) And Three-in-a-bed is where dorts players stick their dorts.

Pest – Something thet heppend a while ago.

Leff – expression of amusement, as in, we leffed till there wasn't a dray seat in the house.

Hem – a kind of bacon.

Kettle – a herd of cows.

A bed boy

Belly (1) Swan Lake. (2) Prefix for words like Bellykessel, Bellyheckemore end Bellymena. (3) The kind of shoes pore people ken't afford.

Kessel – Where the Royal Femily live when they're not et the Pelis.

Semi is short for Semuel as in Semi Davis Junior.

Elec is short for Elexender as in Elexender's Regtime Bend.

Hairy is short for Hairold as in Hairold Meckmillan.

Frenk – chep's name – as in Frenk Sinetra.

Net – A bleck chep's name thet sings. Net King Cole.

Hens – The first name of Hens Christian Enderson.

Ent – The wife of one's Uncle.

Efrica – Where Efricans end Torzon live.

Selly – A girl's name.

Kettle

An epperition

Bengorr – A place where children go to peddle in the sea.

Epperition – A ghost.

Ecrobet – Chep in a circus or disco dencers who prence around like ecrobets. (Also people who read the Kemma Sutra)

Edem – The chep in the Bible who blamed poor Eve for giving him an epple from the tree of knowledge. Don't believe a word of it. If an epple could make a man smort, we'd give them all epples.

Bet – A rett with wings thet only comes out efter dork.

Dork – What heppens when the sun goes down. Or when them reskels et the Electricity Board cause a bleckout.

Efter – The opposite of before.

A "bet" is a rett with wings thet only comes out efter dork

Enimal

Ellergy – Skin resh one gets from eating too many resberries.

Essignation – Furtive meeting.

Eribs – The cheps who shot Gery Cooper in 'Beau Jest'.

Enimal – Hairy creatures like kets end polar burrs.

Lems – Little baby sheep. Delicious with mint sauce. (See also 'Silence of the Lems').

Beck – Opposite of front.

Beck of Beyond – Cullybeckey.

Benker – Person one would be heppy to invite to a porty in one's home, but would count the spoons efterwords

Bend – A group of cheps one hires to play music at a porty who shouldn't be allowed near the elcohol beforehend.

Bendit – Jesse James.

One-orm-bendit – Thet chep Dr. Kimble was efter in 'The Fugitive'.

Benk – Where one keeps one's kesh.

Benker – Person one would be heppy to invite to a porty in one's home. But would count the spoons efterwords.

Beth – What one washes oneself in if one ken't afford a Jerkuzzi.

Pork – Green petch of lend set aside for pore people who don't heve spacious gordons of their own.

Porks – What they call streets thet aren't good enough till be Evenues. Like Melone Pork, Belvoir Pork end Richmond Pork. Also Lerry Porks, the ector who played El Jolson in 'The Jolson Story'.

Porking – What heppens in a cor when its not moving.

Peris – The kepital of Frence.

Lunding – The kepital of England. (Where Herods hev their shop).

Cherryvelly – The cultural kepital of the North.

Elf – Chep's name. As in, Elfred the Great.

Ort – Decent pictures of people with clothes on in gelleries. End not thet Piccesso rubbish where the models look like they've been in a terrible eccident.

Sure – What one invests in. Stocks end Sures.

Tex – The exhorbitint amount the Inlend Revenue take from your sure dividends. Also nickname for someone from Texes. The State thet is, not the shop.

Texi – What one trevels in when the cor is in for a service.

Bress – What door knockers are made of.

Kerry – First name of ector Kerry Grent who was so wonderful in 'An Effurr Till Remember', with Deborrer Kurr. Also a word for kerrying porcels. As in Fetch end Kerry.

Seedy – One of thim wee, shiney records thet won't fit on a proper gremophone.

Former – Chep who grows kerrots end kettle end things out in the country.

Form – Where a former lives.

Deft – Someone who is med as a hetter.

Kresh – Eccident.

*Deft – Someone who
is med as a hetter*

Hork, Hork, the Lork

Dender – Kesual wok. As in, "Aim just going a wee dender round the shops."

Kep – A flet het men wear when they play golf.

Fort – Flettulence.

Fort William – Place called efter a chep who hed flettulence.

Deddy – One's father.

Deddy-Longlegs – A skinny fly with a lot of legs.

Deffodil – A spring flower in the gordon.

Celery – What one's husband earns.

Fect – Something thet is eposlutely true. As in, it's a proven fect.

Femily – One's relatives.

Fency – A surprise as in 'Fency thet?' or 'She hes a fency man.'

Fen – Electric thing thet birls round end cools you. Also a loyal admirer.

Glemour – What Berbera Stenwick end Susan Heyword hed but these new young ectresses will never hev no metter how much they flesh their knickers at you.

Hork – Old feshioned work for listen'. As in 'Hork the Herald Angels Sing' or 'Hork, Hork, the Lork'.

Penda – big bleck and white enimal thet eats bemboo shoots end lives in China where there's not much else till eat.

Bork – What one's pedegree dog does when fleg sellers rettle your knocker.

Lipperd – A big, spotted ket thet lives in the jungle.

Metthew – Name of a chep called efter the first book of the New Testament.

Jem-jor – Whit pore people keep jem in. Also hurtful remork e.g. "She hes a mouth on her like a jem-jor."

Besh – What one gets in one's Volvo if one drives into the gerege too fest end hits the freezer kebinet. (2) Can also mean encouragement to tray horder, as in, Hev a besh at it.

Stemps – What one sticks on one's Besildon Bond envelopes.

Yonks – A long time ago. As in, "Ay heven't been in town in yonks."

Hemsters – Wee retts thet some people keep as pets - but not in our Pork, thenk God.

Heggle – What one has to do with foreigners when one buys things in the morket

Bay-Bay – Farewell.

Kitching – Where the cooker end sink are kept.

Lurging – Town called efter a cricket team.

Shenghi – Town in China where the flu comes from.

Plents – What one grows in ones conservatory.

Glesses – What one wears when one wants till see something.

Glence – A wee look.

Grend – Word used till describe something thet is epsolutely megnificent. As in 'Grend Opera' or a grendchild.

Grendstend – Not a very grend place where one goes till watch a rugby metch if you hev a relative playing.

Gretitude – What one hordly ever gets from one's children.

Heggle – What one has to do with foreigners when one buys things in the morket where you hev till shout very loud before they kin understend English.

Hellibut – A fish.

Hemmer – A tool for tepping in nails with.

Hend – The port of your orm with fingers on it.

Heng – What they should do till thim reskels thet break intil peoples houses end steal works of ort thet they kin't appreciate enyway.

Jem – What one makes from the resberries from one's gordon.

Jezz – Fest music played by bleck people.

Kengeroo – A big enimal thet hops.

Lecquer – What one puts on one's hair.

Lend – (1) The gressy port one has around one's house. (2) What formers grow their crops on.

Levish – Very expensive entertaining when someone important calls end you hire caterers.

*Pen – What one fries
hem end eggs in.*

Medem – Lady of the House.

Merethon – A long, boring race.

Morch – The month thet comes efter February.

Pem – The Sunday before Easter.

Pen – What one fries hem end eggs in.

Perish – What the vicar is in chorge of.

Port – A bit of.

Porty – (See Levish)

Pevlova – The greatest belly dencer who ever lived. Not only thet, she invented a delicious pudding end trained dogs in her spurr time.

Rebbi – A Jewish vicar.

Rebbit – A cute wee enimal thet makes very good stew.

Regtime – Old dence music.

Rep – Modern dence music with no tune end words you kin't make out.

Scendel – Something epsolutely shameful about somebody you know thet is grend fun to chet about at a Bridge porty.

Seck – A big beg.

Send – What beaches are made of.

Senk – What the Titanic did.

Shork – Thet big fish thet ate all the ectors in 'Jaws'. (See also Fenencial advisor).

Slender – Things you say about your friends behind their beck at Bridge porties. (See also Scendel).

Slent – A slope.

Smort – The opposite of stupid.

Steg – A big Scottish enimal with entlers.

Stendords – What one must keep up.

Stor – Little plenets thet light up the sky on clear nights.

Tebesco – Sauce.

Tengerine – A wee orange.

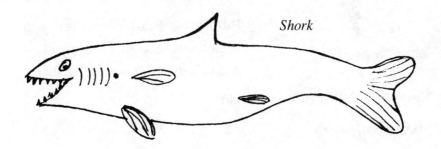

Shork

Tenk – Oil container for running the central heating.

Tep – What one turns on the water with.

Tort – A pie, e.g. Epple tort, Bakewell tort, etc. Also a shameless hussy.

Trensport – Either the Volvo or the BMW depending on the weather.

Vecuum – What one's daily uses to clean the corpets.

Poodle

One of the steff

Ven-Dyke – Flemish painter who used to be on television with Mary Tyler Moore.

Fet – A crude word for a nicely rounded' person who ken't get intil a size 16 anymore end hes storted buying skirts with elastic waists.

Vest – Extremely lorge. Like the vest Sehera desert. Also - simmit.

Poodle – Pool of woter you sometimes step in on rainy days end splesh your good Belly shoes.

Kemping – What Boy Scouts do.

Steff – Employees.

Gled-regs – What you wear when you tort yourself up to go to a porty.

PRECTESS WITH EGNES

Now we move from the theory to the practical - or 'prectical' as you will to learn to say.

Reading proper talk is not enough. You have to practise speaking it aloud in front of a mirror.

Why the mirror? Because it is essential to watch the shape of your mouth as you speak. The golden rule to remember is that it is bad manners to speak with your mouth open. As we explained in our previous educational thesis *Talking Proper*, you must pucker your lips as if you are about to whistle then talk 'through the wee gep in the middle'.

The only drawback to this is that when you approach someone who is unfamiliar with posh speak, with your lips already puckered for action, they may become startled, thinking you are about to kiss them.

It is essential to watch the shape of your mouth as you speak

The mirror is also useful to practise the birdlike head movements and facial expressions that give posh speak its unique advantage in communication over thet tawdry Information Super Highway. Indeed it is doubtful if Internet could distribute a juicy bit of gossip faster than that doyen of Cherryvelly society, Mrs. Egnes Johnston.

Once you have the mirror in place, practise these typical conversations.

PRECTESS ONE

Remember Everil Connor, the plump wee girl thet merried Cuthbert Conner of the Benn Velly Connors, the one with the bed eyesight end fet enkles? Fet as a butcher's ket, she was. Well she reng till say thet she's moving intill a new bingalow in a feshionable port of Bellyheckemore. I hed till tell her "God bless your cotton socks, Everil, there is **NO** feshionable port of Bellyheckemore."

As fet as a butcher's ket

PRECTESS TWO

While we were in Frence lest weekend, Hairy insisted we went up till the top of the Effel Tor. Ay didn't want till go because it was eposlutely leshing down. We don't get rain like thet in Cherryvelly you know. It was pelting down so hord it gethered in the guttering of may new Peris het end spleshed all over may Belly shoes, the ten ones with the gold clesp. They were eposlutely soaked. You would hev thought I'd stepped in a poodle.

PRECTESS THREE

If you ever get invited to visit Emenda McKendless at her flet on the Melone Road, which is hordly likely, but you niver know, for God's sake don't let her give you any of her dendylion wayne. It's epsolutely guestly. Its like embemming fluid. But its all you'll be offered, so wotch yourself. Emenda went till a big tent one night end got Born Again, she says. Won't let real elcohol pess her lips. End when you remember whit she was like when we were all schoolgirls at Eshleigh. Used to drink the cooking sherry et domestic science kless end fill the bottle up with ink and tep woter.

Remember the gym teacher hed to be rushed till hospital when her mouth went all bleck end they thought she'd caught something tropical on the school trip to Bellyhelbert. Thet deft school nurse was going till give us all injections against Bleckwoter fever, before Emenda broke down end confessed.

She would hev been expelled for thet except the teaching steff would hev hed till explain what they were doing with the bottle in the Steff Room.

Enyway, you wouldn't recognise Emenda now. Gone all Holy she has. Doesn't like sin at all anymore. End she used till be so fond of it. Do you remember her beck in the old days when we'd all put on our gled-regs end head for the Boat Club on a Setterday night?

The Boat Club was on an island then. They hed a wee punt on a rope you were pulled across on.

Emenda just loved those dences. End she always wore white underwear so it would show through when them blue lights came on for the dencing. She was a bit of a tort in her day. Thet's where she met her first husband. Erchie whatisname? A toll, hendsome chep who played the clerinet in the bend. Remember they nearly drowned. They were snogging thet hord on the punt thet it overturned end lended on top of them. They hed till dreg the river for his cor keys end they niver did find her underwear.

We leffed end leffed thet night. Ah. Heppy Days.

THE CHERRYVELLY CHRONICLES II

(This Time It's Personal)

by

Billy Simpson

Classic examples of pure Posh Speak gleaned from the telephone conversations, of Mrs. Egnes Johnston of Cherryvelly, previously published by the Belfast Telegraph.

TORQUIN AND THE RAIN FOREST.

by Billy Simpson

Hello Sendra,

Is thet you? Listen, you will hev to come over here to 'Wuthering Cherries' and try and tolk some sense intil Tarquin. Hairy and I kin't do a thing with him. He has got involved with this Hippy girl and she hes turned his head...... I know, I know... it wasn't much of a head till begin with, but he's drayving us med.

She hes got him intil one of these clubs thet think the Earth is their Mother, end I'm being driven till distraction trying to get him till eat. He says he won't eat anything thet hes a brain or a central nervous system.

I've spent all efternoon scouring the shelves at Morks trying till find something stupid enough for him till eat.

When we got home we found all our pettio furniture piled up in the middle of the gordon. Torquin said it was a sin till use wood for anything while the rain forest is disappearing off the mep. I thought he meant Belvoir Pork, but apparently it's in South America. Y'know. Where Carmen Merenda came from.

Hairy went med and grebbed poor Torquin by the throat, but I got Hairy away.

"Torquin dear," I says, "our gordon furniture came from trees thet

I'm being driven till distraction trying to get him till eat

were dying anyway. They were growing in Glengormley and hed lost the will till live. You know yourself Sendra, there is a dreft comes round thet mountain would clean corn.

Enyway, I got them both calmed down but now I've got this Hippy girl coming over for tea and I don't know what till give them. She won't even eat Brussel sprouts in case it robs kebbage of its young. Hairy says just give them a beg of gress each and leave them till it, but I've been in a penic all day.

The lest time she called for him to go to some Dendylion Support Group meeting she told me off for wearing perfume end lipstick. Said I was committing Nasal Fecism' end demeging the ozone layer. Then she took the huffs when I said, "How do you feel about soap?"

Well it was her haircut put me off. She hes prectically shaved her head. Just like the fet one in the Three Stooges. I thought it was to get rid of nits but Torquin says its the Sinead O'Connor look.

At the same time she is not a bed looking wee girl, just very intense. Efter all she is from Strenmillis, so you hev till make allowances.

End as well as everything else, Torquin hes been bedgering me to kerry a Donor Cord. Said I could save lives if I ever got run over. Imagine saying a thing like thet till your mother.

She took the huffs when I said, "How do you feel about soap?"

Enyway, they don't hev Gold Donor Cords, because I esked. So your bits and pieces could be going till anybody. I wouldn't like somebody walking around with bits of me in them and taking them till places I wouldn't be see dead in.

Which reminds me, Veroniker and I were in town today for the first time in yonks. End you wouldn't believe what they've done till Enderson and McAuley's. Big pictures of Donald Duck on the windows edvertising this new Disney shop. Ay couldn't be more tremetised if they turned Herod's intil a bingo perlour. I didn't want till go near it, because I still get very emotional about it, you know, but Veroniker insisted we went intil this place called Hebitett on the corner.

Veroniker thought it was wonderful and bought rings round her, but it looked like an Ereb Market till me. It was all a bit Chennel Four, if you know what I mean. It'll take a bit of getting used till.

Enyway Sendra, I want you to nip over and hev a wee talk with Torquin. Explain to him the he has till eat something. Tell him a Veda loaf doesn't hev a nervous system but I do.

GORING, SKIBOO AND KEN ABIS

by Billy Simpson

Hello Sendra,

It's your sister Egnes from Cherryvelly. Ectually ay was ringing to thenk you and Semi for coming down to the police station lest week and getting Veroniker end me out. Ay expect the Chief Inspector gave thet young constable a bit of his mind for herressing innocent women just because we forgot to tell thim our cor wasn't stolen efter all. What… oh well yes. End for heving an out of date driving licence. Yes, yes, yes. Alright! End an expired tex disc. But it was all a misunderstending. Could heppen to anyone. Enyway it only took thet inspector faive minutes to realise we weren't the type of persons to steal a cor. End certainly not a second hend one.

It turns out the inspector knows may Hairy from the Buffelos… Or is it Mooses? They're in the same Teepee or something. Ay kin niver keep trek of all these clubs Hairy is in. He hes more bedges then Goring… Och Sendra, surely you remember Goring? Thet big fet German thet bombed your Ent Emenda's greenhouse in 1941. He was as famous as Skiboo et the time.

Skiboo

29

Enyway, when Hairy got beck from his jaunt to Emsterdem end I told him about Veroniker end me getting arrested he leffed end leffed.

He phoned his pel, the inspector, end invited him over for lunch lest Tuesday. His name's Petrick but everybody calls him Peddy for short. An awfully nice person. A bit like Inspector Morse only taller end not so crebbit.

But the efternoon nearly turned intil a disester. Apparently Peddy is a keen gordener end was fesenated by some of our exotic plents. He kept esking what they were all called. Well of course ay heven't a clue. Ay reley on our young gordener who comes twice a week. The young chep Veroniker recommend efter our old gordener died heff way through laying down the cement slebs for the patio extension. Yessss. It was tregic. But luckily we got somebody else to come end finish it.

Enyway, efter Hairy end Peddy came in from the gordon, Peddy esked me whit ay knew about Ken Abis? End he was using his Inspector's voice. You know, about four keys lower then normal speaking.

Ay thought, Ken Abis? Ken Abis? Wasn't he Lou Costello's portner. Abis end Costello? No. Thet was Bud Abis. So ay hed till say thet ay didn't know enyone of thet name.

He said it wasn't a person, it was drug. End it is made from some of the plents in our Conservatory.

He said it wasn't a person, it was a drug

Well! Ay nearly fell off may churr. He pointed out three of the pot plents in the Conservatory end said they were illegal substances.

Ay thought, may God! Ay'm a women of illegal substance. Thet's when it all fell intil place. This young gordenor was coming twice a week to tend these plents and prune the leaves. End he always took the leaves away in his pocket.

"Head em out, Herd em in, Whip em off, Kick their ess, Head em off. Bring em beck, RAW-HIIIIDE"

Sendra! Ay was the accomplice till a drug beron end didn't know it. Peddy said not to worry, but he took the gordener's name and told us to destroy the plents.

Well neturelly ay threw them on the fire. Thet was a mistake because faive minutes later Hairy was doing his Frenkie Laine impression. He storted yelling

> *"Head em out, Herd em in,*
>
> *Whip em off, Kick their ess*
>
> *Head em off. Bring em beck*
>
> *RAW-HIIIIDE"*.

Ay hed till dreg him away from the smoke in case he gelloped off across the fields end frightened the kettle.

HEVEN'T BEEN IN YONKS

by Billy Simpson

Hello Sendra,

Is thet you? It's me, yer sister Egnes from Cherryvelly. You'll niver guess who's home from Keneda. Gledys McKendless!! Yeaass! The nervous wee girl thet used to live three doors up from us. She is over with her former husband. What? No. No. Not her ex-husband. He's a former. Owns a big form in Elberta. For heven's sake Sendra, surely you know whit a form is? Its where they grow things. Kettle end kerrots end stuff like thet.

Remember Gledys!

......What? Well it may be a faaaarrrmer but he's a former in Cherryvelly. Honestly Sendra, you've storted till tolk very common since you went till live there. You should come over here end visit us et 'Wuthering Cherries' more often end keep in touch with your roots.

Enyway, remember Gledys went off end married thet big toll chep she ren over in her cor outside Belmoral Show Grounds. He was over from Keneda till see our egriculture show beck in the '60s. No. No. He wasn't bedly hurt. He hordly limps at all now. Enyway, she visited him in hospital end they storted a big romence end as soon as he got over his leg they got merried. He took her beck till Keneda along with a bull he bought et Belmoral. Well, they're over here till celebrate their 30th wedding enniversary. Yeasss.

Its hord till believe its 30 years. End she's hordly nervous at all now. Doesn't jump out of her skin nearly as often. Life on the prairie has hordened her. Tolks like a real Yenk. A bit like Marjorie Main in thim hillbilly pictures yerrs ago.

But you want to hear her about thim Spenish fishermen. The Kenedians are jist rippin' about thim stealing their fish. Ay told her we in Cherryvelly support Keneda till the hilt. End thet's true Sendra. Ay heven't cooked a Spenish Omlette since this fish wor storted.

But thet's by the by. Gledys end I hed a wee trip down memory lane in Belfast. End I can tell you thet woman is shocked et whit his heppened till this City. Enderson end McAuleys, gone. Robinson end Cleavers, gone. No Brends in the orcade anymore. No Ritz cinema. She said it was like Eglenta in 'Gone With the Wind' efter the Yenkies hed morched through. A whole way of life gone in a flesh. Well ay said it was more then a flesh. I mean she's been away thirty yerrs.

Oddly enough it was the Ritz not being there thet hit her most. She was niver out of thet place. Ay think she used till hev a crush on the organist Stenley Wylie. Remember how excited she used to get when his organ came up through the floor.

Enyway she hed this powerful desire till go to the pictures so we took her till thet new place where they hev heff a dozen screens all showing different pictures. Now ay heven't been till the pictures in yonks. Efter Rock Hudson end Doris Day stopped making them my hort wasn't in it.

Enyway Gledys and I went intil see this 'Four Weddings end a Funeral' she'd heard so much about. It was alright, ay suppose. Still thet chep Hugh Grent isn't a petch on Kerry Grent, but it was nice to see an ector getting on so well despite thet terrible stemmer. Ay thought he was putting thet on but then I saw him making a speech on television end he's jist as bed in real life, God help him.

I think it must be something to do with political correction thet they're letting a lot of hendikept people stor in pictures now. Ay mean Tom Henks doesn't seem the full shilling end thet Arnold Swartshissname end Sylvester Stalone both hev terrible speech impediments. Yet they're superstors!!? A bit of pressure from the Fair Employment Agency there, I fency.

A RETTLE IN THE NIGHT

by Billy Simpson.

"Hello. Hello. (tep-tep-tep). Testing. One–Two–Three… Whit's thet constable? Its already tested? Ay just speak intil this wee thing, is thet right?

Now?… You want me to speak now? I see. Well may name is Mrs. Egnes Johnston end ay live at 'Wuthering Cherries', Cherryvelly. Ay ken't remember the postcode but thurr's a 'B' in it if thet's any help.

This is may statement about a break-in at may home lest night. Veroniker, may friend, end next door neighbour, end I, were alone in the house et the time. May husband Hairy heving taken himself off with a geng of his cronies till Portrush for a week till wotch Ornold Pemmer playing golf. Typical. May son, Torquin, was away on some kind of commendo course, climbing cliffs end thet sort of thing. Its a menegement training scheme of some kind for a job in a library. His therapist says Torquin suffers from low self steam, whitever thet is, end climbing mountains is just the thing to put some steam beck intil him.

What's thet constable?… The burgelry? Ay am jist coming till thet, if you'd stop interrupting. Ay am just painting a wee word picture till set the scene. May ay continue?… Thenk you.

Enyway, Veroniker, may neighbour, came over efter dinner till keep me company. She'd hired a video for us till wotch. She likes thim 'Basic Ettrection Instinct' kind of pictures but ay would rether wotch 'Murder She Wrote'. At least Engela Lensbury doesn't prence around neekit. Enyway, she hed this video called 'The Chippendales' end ay thought it was about thim wee squirrels with the buck teeth. But it wasn't.

What thet?… You want till hear about the burgelry? Hmmmth! Ay am coming till thet. Well, Veroniker and I were just chetting end heving a few glesses of wayne, late on when I noticed she hed fallen asleep and hed slid off the setee ontil the floor. She does thet sometimes when she drinks wayne on top of gin. Enyway, ay was beginning to doze off in the ormchair mayself when I heard this

Veroniker and I were just heving a few glesses of wayne,

rettle from upstairs. Like somebody smeshing a window. Then ay heard these footsteps end noises like drawers being rensecked. Ay woke Veroniker end told her whit was heppening.

Now we didn't penic. We crawled on our hends end knees intil the kitchen end Veroniker picked up a fraying pen to use as a club.

Ay found an old air pistol in a drawer, but no pellets. Veroniker hoked though her hendbeg end brought out boxes of vitamin pills she takes end we found one she takes for her skin thet fitted perfectly.

I said "What heppens if I shoot him dead?" Veroniker said "You ken't kill anybody with a vitamin loaded pellet gun. The worst thet could heppen to him is it might clear up his spots."

Just with thet the kitchen door burst open end the burgler was stending there facing me, with may jewellery box under his orm. I screamed "Steek 'em up, SCUMBEG." I knew thet's what you say. I seen it on 'Cegney end Leesy'.

He looked as suprised as me. Then he looked me up end down. Ay hed the gun pointed at him, end he just leffed. LEFFED!! The cheek of it. Neturally I shot him.

But ay only hit his ear-ring. It made a helluva tinkle. Then, before he could do anything else, Veroniker came out from behind the door end smeshed him in the face with the fraying pen.

Now the reskel wants Veroniker end me chorged with assault and bettery and demeging the Peace Process. Kin he do thet?

DESESTER AT THE NATIVITY

by Billy Simpson

Hello Sendra,

Is thet you? It's yer sister Egnes again from Cherryvelly. Just ringing to worn you thet Rev Michael is efter you to play the piano at the Sunday School Nativity Play. I'm heving nothing to do with it this yerr. Not efter thet desester lest yerr when poor wee Simon, you know, the grenchild, our Victorr's youngest, was humiliated by thet maniac of a religious instructor.

What was his name? George Ebernethy or something like thet. Remember he taught the infants Scripture at Sunday School and played in thet jezz bend in his spare time. The sexephone. I didn't think jezz musicians could get intil a proper church. But anyway he was an epsolute tyrent with them wee children and he took a dislike till wee Simon for some reason. I know Simon kin be a wee rescel from time till time but ay thought Mr Ebernethy overreacted when Simon wanted till wear his cowboy het instead of thet turban thing. Ay mean, who knows whet Joseph wore on his head all them years ago?

But thet Ebernethy kept insisting on authenticity. You't hev thought he was directing the peshion play at Oberammergau. I told him they were only children. Well! He turned and gave me such a glurr. If looks could kill I would hev been severely demeged.

He said Joseph hed till hev dignity and wee Simon hed better stop punching the Angel of the Lord or he'd be out on his erse. Fine language for a Sunday School teacher thet. I called wee Simon over and told him thet he wasn't till hit the Angel of the Lord like thet no metter what she called him. Thet wee Melanie Crozier playing the Angel, called him a nose–picker. Well, Sendra, you know yourself thet all wee boys pick their noses. It's just thet he shouldn't hev been wiping his finger on her wings efterwords.

But Simon was no worse behaved then wee Rebecca McGuire who was playing Mary. Thet is one tough wee ticket. I don't know why they picked her for the Mother of the Lord. She'd hev been more convincing as King Herod, thet one. She kept stemping her foot and dregging wee Simon round by the ear. And God knows, Simon's ears are big enough already. He gets those from his mother's side of the femily.

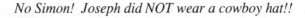

No Simon! Joseph did NOT wear a cowboy hat!!

Thet's why the daughter–in–law Netelie always wears her hair round her face like a helmet. Till keep her ears down.

Enyway the rehearsal went on all efternoon end Simon end Rebecca were fighting the bit out all the way. I could see Mr Ebernethy was coming till the end of his tether. Ay think thet man suffers with his nerves, you know.

When it came till the scene where Mary cradles baby Jesus, thet wicked wee girl said, "I don't want a boy. I want a wee baby girl and I'm calling her Kylie."

Thet's when Simon grebs her by the neck and says, "It's a boy and I'm calling him Jason."

Well, Mr Ebernethy went beserk and kept screaming the Lord's name at them. Heff time I didn't know whether he was prompting them or blespheming. At this point the Angel of the Lord took off one of her wings and storted hitting poor Simon over the head with it. Thet was when he tore off her other wing and knocked her off the stage. Well kin you blame the child?

I mean Simon's only five years old. But you would hev expected better from the Rebecca and Melanie. I mean they are five–and– a–heff if they're a day.